AF583824

For Percy, Mabel, and Matt, always
And for you, Gigi
Yvette

To Randy,
My partner, best friend,
and biggest supporter
Chloe

It is important that in the place and space you find yourself, to please stop in your tracks as we walk on Mother Earth, and take a moment to pay respects to the Traditional Custodians, both past and present, and honour their profound connection with this land. Join us on a journey to uncover the enchanting lessons nature has in store for our adventurous hearts.

Duane Byrnes
A First Nations descendant from Wonnarua Country,
living on Dharawal Country

Nature Knows

Yvette Farmer & Chloe Jasmine Harris

2
1

Sometimes our house gets busy.

Really busy.

Mum calls this feeling foofy.

Dad calls it time-to-go-camping!

55

Nature knows how to calm our minds with sound. When we listen to leaves rustling, birds singing and water trickling, the calm part of our brains gently awakens, which helps us feel relaxed.

We arrive when the wind is settling, and the daytime birds are singing their last songs. We stand outside and listen.

Dad says you can listen with more than your ears.

My feet can hear the passage of ants, my skin listens to the trees talking,

even the misty air has something to say.

When the sun goes down, we sit by the warm fire.

Sometimes we are loud,

mostly we are quiet.

Nature knows when it's time to rest. Watching the warm yellows and oranges of the setting sun sends a message to our brains to slow down. Feeling the warmth of a camp fire, with its crackling sounds and smoky smell, gives our bodies the signal to drift towards sleep.

I like waking up in our tent.
It's like being outside inside,
and that makes my inside and outside
feel pretty good somehow.

Nature knows how to set up our body clocks for the day. Being outside in the morning sunshine when we first wake up helps us feel alert and makes us feel happier.

When we get up, Mum makes tea on the fire.

Our baby feels the dirt.

I play with a stick.

Nature knows that playing in the dirt keeps us happy and healthy. Getting a bit grubby makes our immune systems strong and stops us getting sick.

We don't do a lot.

But it's full, and real, and special.

Nature knows that when we spend time doing simple things, like smelling flowers or watching a river flow, it makes us feel happier and more connected with the natural world.

'Can you feel this?' asks Mum,

'The gentle breeze across your skin, the hum of insect song?'

She tells me to let it all in,

that nature knows how to bring us back to ourselves.

I lay down and think
but it doesn't really feel like thinking,
it feels like knowing...
that we *are* nature and nature is us.

The wind is the air in my lungs,
the river is my blood.
The rocks and the earth are my bones
and the fire is my heart.

The mud on my skin is messy,
the rain can wash it away.
It's not neat here, or in order,
the trees don't grow in straight lines.

But there is room,
for *all* of me.

When it's time to pack up, I don't want to go home.

But Dad says I can carry this feeling with me anywhere.

Nature knows how to stay with us. Even after we leave, we can remember the wind in the trees and the dirt beneath our feet . . . reminding us it's time to go camping again soon.

So I do.

I breathe it in.

I hold it right next to my heart.

I bring it home.

It helps me on the busy days.

Scientists have been exploring how nature makes us feel and behave, and have found out some pretty cool facts. Being in nature can help us calm down, focus, feel good and even spark our creativity.

Maybe you love climbing trees or skipping rocks in a river. Maybe you like exploring in the bush or swimming at the beach. Wherever you are, nature is waiting for you . . . what can you discover?

Find something...

the same colour as your eyes

that's fresh and new

you can draw or make a mark with

that flutters

that fits snugly in your palm

that's very old

that makes a song

that smells sweet

that tickles

that can hold water

that feels smooth

YVETTE FARMER is a writer and teacher. She has also worked as a researcher at the University of Western Sydney, exploring the positive effects nature can have on a child's wellbeing. Yvette lives an hour south of Sydney between the escarpment and the sea and goes camping with her family whenever she can.

CHLOE JASMINE HARRIS studied Fine Arts at the National Art School. Her illustration style reflects her love for the outdoors and the little creatures she finds along the way. She is particularly fond of mossy rainforests, hidden caves and the ocean after a storm.

First published in Australia in 2026
by Thames & Hudson Australia
Wurundjeri Country, 132A Gwynne Street,
Cremorne, Victoria 3121

First published in the United States of America in 2026
by Thames & Hudson Inc.
500 Fifth Avenue
New York, New York 10110

29 28 27 26 5 4 3 2 1

ISBN 978-1-760-76529-3
ISBN 978-1-760-76580-4 (U.S. edition)

A catalogue record for this book is available from the National Library of Australia

Library of Congress Control Number 2025947159

Cover illustration: Chloe Jasmine Harris
Cover design: Andy Warren & Casey Schuurman
Design: Andy Warren & Casey Schuurman
Printed and bound in China by C&C Offset Printing Co., Ltd

Thames & Hudson Australia wishes to acknowledge that Aboriginal and Torres Strait Islander peoples are the first storytellers of this nation and the Traditional Custodians of the land on which we live and work. We acknowledge their continuing culture and pay respect to Elders past and present.

thamesandhudson.com.au
thamesandhudson.com
thamesandhudsonusa.com